Credit Overhaul

Repair Your Finances, Lower Your Debt & Grow Your Credit Score

A Simple Guide to Improve Your Financial Wellbeing and Free Yourself from Money Stress

Nicholas Patrick

© **Copyright 2019 by Nicholas Patrick - All rights reserved.**

This document is geared towards providing exact and reliable information in regards to the topic and issue covered. The publication is sold with the idea that the publisher is not required to render accounting, officially permitted, or otherwise, qualified services. If advice is necessary, legal or professional, a practiced individual in the profession should be ordered.

- From a Declaration of Principles which was accepted and approved equally by a Committee of the American Bar Association and a Committee of Publishers and Associations.

In no way is it legal to reproduce, duplicate, or transmit any part of this document in either electronic means or in printed format. Recording of this publication is strictly prohibited and any storage of this document is not allowed unless with written permission from the publisher. All rights reserved.

The information provided herein is stated to be truthful and consistent, in that any liability, in terms of inattention or otherwise, by any usage or abuse of any policies, processes, or directions contained within is the solitary and utter responsibility of the recipient reader. Under no circumstances will any legal responsibility or blame be held against the publisher for any reparation, damages, or monetary loss due to the information herein, either directly or indirectly.

Respective authors own all copyrights not held by the publisher.

The information herein is offered for informational purposes solely and is universal as so. The presentation of the information is without contract or any type of guarantee assurance.

The trademarks that are used are without any consent, and the publication of the trademark is without permission or backing by the trademark owner. All trademarks and brands within this book are for clarifying purposes only and are the owned by the owners themselves, not affiliated with this document.

Table of Contents

Introduction v

Chapter 1: Understand Your Present Financial State 1

Chapter 2: The Secret Is Budgeting 7

Chapter 3: Improve Your Credit Score 15

Chapter 4: Repay Debt, Improve Your Credit Score, and Become Financially Free 21

Chapter 5: Start Building Wealth 27

Chapter 6: Align Your Mindset 33

Conclusion 39

Bonus: Checklist 43

Introduction

I want to thank you and congratulate you for buying *"Credit Overhaul: Repair Your Finances, Lower Your Debt & Grow Your Credit Score."*

This book contains proven steps and strategies that when implemented, will help you take control of your financial wellbeing.

If you are in debt right now, you know how excessively burdensome it can feel. Bad debt can debilitate your financial life and living from one paycheck to the next can be extremely stressful. It can also keep you from achieving your dreams and aspirations.

In addition to increasing your stress and anxiety and keeping you from achieving your financial goals and living your best life, being in bad debt can also have very significant negative effects on your credit score, or rather, your "credit worthiness."

This book will talk about why you should care about your credit score and if you already have a poor credit score, how to overhaul your credit by budgeting and repaying your debt in a systematic, gradual manner that allows you to build good credit.

This book shall discuss important elements of the "debt free" process, i.e. how to go from being in debt and having a bad credit score, to being debt free, financially stable, and consistently working towards your financial goals.

Among other things, I will discuss:

1. Everything you have ever wanted to know about your credit score
2. How bad debt affects your life
3. Budgeting, its benefits, and how to create a budget that works for you
4. How to get started on the "getting out of debt" process
5. And how to get started on your journey to financial freedom

If you diligently implement the ideas you distill from this book, your financial life will greatly improve and will never be the same again.

Thanks again for buying this book. I hope you enjoy it!

Chapter 1:

Understand Your Present Financial State

Why do you want to get out of debt? Is it because you want to feel more in control of your financial life? Is it because you are tired of living from paycheck to paycheck? Is it because you want to start improving your credit score so that you can get better loan and mortgage terms? Is it because you want to cultivate a better relationship with money or to get started on the path to financial freedom?

To win over debt, the motive behind your goal <u>has to be a personal 'must'</u>. If the factors driving your desire to take control of your finances are not personal imperatives attached with the committed desire to change your situation, you are unlikely to take the actions necessary to create financial stability that will result in a life of abundance.

Take a moment to think about why you want to get out of debt. On the surface, getting out of debt will improve your life in so many ways. Perhaps, at a minimum, you want to get out of debt so that you manage how much you earn and how much you spend in order to allocate your money from one month to the next depending on your financial goals and aims.

Perhaps you want to get out of debt so that you can have peace of mind each month in knowing that you have enough money to cover your basic needs and still have enough funds left over to save, invest, and maybe indulge a bit. Perhaps you want to get out of debt so that you can get started on saving towards your dream home, wedding, vacation, car, experience, etc.

Make sure that the factors driving your desire to become debt free and financially stable are well-defined and personal 'musts' because the process of getting out of debt can often times be arduous and challenging depending on your present debt level and financial state. The stronger your WHY, the more the likelihood of sticking with the process and from it, yield great results!

Now that you have pinpointed your ultimate reason for wanting to get out of debt, gain more control over your finances, and get started on the path to financial freedom, you need to understand something of crucial importance:

Good vs. Bad Debt

Depending on how much you earn each month and the different expense allocation buckets your income has to fill each month, you will be pleased to know that it is possible to live a completely debt free life. Ultimately, all you really need to do is *"live within your means— spend less than you earn—save, and invest in profitable ventures."* The more consistently you are able to do this, the faster you will realize financial success.

The word debt often has negative connotations attached to it. While often seen as negative, debt is not always bad; you can also have good debt. Establishing a distinction between the two is important.

A poor credit score is often a result of bad debt, or rather, excessive spending on depreciating assets (i.e. assets that lose their value with use or over time). For instance, using your credit card to shop for clothes, services, electronics, travel and other items that satisfy your immediate desires is bad debt because what you are essentially doing is buying things that will neither generate income nor appreciate in value (e.g. assets).

When you borrow money to invest in appreciating assets such as a business, your education, a house, your self-betterment, etc. you are getting into good debt; good debt is any money borrowed and directed towards income generating ventures of any nature.

One key thing to note about good debt is that getting it normally requires good credit. This means if you have bad credit, accruing any form of debt, including good debt, will be problematic because your credit score is the primary factor lenders look at when determining whether you are credit worthy—capable of repaying the debt—and the interest to affix to the debt.

Since both of these debts (good and bad) can take many shapes and forms, determining whether a debt is good or bad boils down to your present financial life and aims. You should always aim to accrue good debt and to avoid (or minimize) bad debt at all costs. If you have already accrued some bad debts, you should know that they are affecting your credit score negatively, and you should therefore take immediate action to rectify the matter by creating an effective debt free plan.

A latter section of this guide will help you create a debt free plan that works for you.

Since bad debt is the primary cause of bad credit, let's talk a bit more about bad credit.

How a poor credit scores affects your life

The ultimate definition of a poor credit score or "bad credit" is "a displayed failure to keep up with your financial obligations." Simplified, having poor credit means you have shown a tendency to borrow money and not keep up with the repayments as promised.

When your credit is poor, because you have displayed a failure to keep up with your payments, lenders and creditors will not trust you and therefore deny you any future loans.

Creditors use your credit score to determine whether to grant you a loan. When your score is low or poor, it essentially tells a lender that you have shown a tendency not to keep up with your financial obligations. What lender would willingly lend money to someone who has shown a clear history of not repaying his or her debts?

Your credit score also affects your mortgage rate. When your credit score is poor, you are extremely likely to pay a higher mortgage rate—if you are lucky enough to find a willing lender; the higher your credit score (740+), the more attractive you are to lenders and the less you are likely to pay more in interest for conventional loans such as mortgages.

Poor credit also influences the interest rate you pay when you do get a loan. Most often, a bad credit score results in higher interest rates—on everything including credit cards, mortgage, car loans, insurance, etc. while a good credit score means favorable interest rates.

A poor credit score has many negative effects on your life, which is why you must commit to repaying your debt as effectively as possible so that you can boldly walk the path to financial stability and freedom.

Ideally you have identified a strong reason for wanting to get out of debt, you know about good and bad debt, and you know about how bad debt and a bad credit score affects different areas of your life. The next chapter outlines the next step you need to implement to be debt free and financially independent.

Chapter 2:

The Secret Is Budgeting

Like debt, budgeting has many negative connotations. Most of us consider budgeting tedious; even though, it doesn't have to be. A budget is simply a tool that allows you to see how much money you earn each month and how you use this income once you receive it.

Budgeting allows you to keep a record of how you are using your income, which, when you are in debt and looking to get out of it, allows you to see exactly what you need to do or stop doing so that you can dedicate more money to becoming debt free and saving more so that you can invest more.

Creating a financial budget is an effective way to feel more in control of your financial present and future. Among many other tangible and intangible benefits, budgeting allows you to:

1. Track your finances and financial aims: To get out of debt, you need to stop spending

money on unnecessary purchases, cut back on expenses where possible, dedicate as much as you can to debt repayment, creating an emergency fund, and saving/investing. A budget allows you to track your finances so that you know when you are living below or above your means depending on your financial situation.
2. Better organize and allocate your money: When you start tracking where your money comes from and where it goes, it becomes easier to see which aspects of your life are using the most money. This knowledge makes it easier to organize your money around your financial goals.
3. Know when something is not going right: Budgeting is an effective warning system for a looming financial crisis in your life. This is because when you know how you spend your money, it becomes easier to connect the financial dots that lead to your ultimate financial dream/future, which makes it easier to foresee financial problems long before they arise.

In addition, when you have a clear budget, you gain a feeling of being in control of your finances. This has the added effect of reducing financial stress and anxiety, and allows you to function at your level best as you work towards your financial goals and creating financial freedom. Further, lower stress around money can affect other areas of your life, such as improving relations with those closest to you.

Budgeting can be as elaborate as you want it to be. You can create spreadsheets, use budgeting apps or software, or create a budget the traditional way: using a pen and paper. Whichever way you do it, the goal is to ensure you create a budget that works for you.

NOTE: Irrespective of which budgeting method you choose to use—and there are many methods—when creating a budget that works for you, keep in mind that the aim is to track your money so that you can see whether you are living below or above your means.

While there are plenty of budgeting tools, applications, free spreadsheets, and software, budgeting is actually very simple. All you really need to do is:

Step 1

To create a budget, the first thing you ought to do is create a system that allows you to track your spending automatically. You can use the traditional method of manually tracking your expenditure by recording everything you purchase within a month, and indeed, having such a record is invaluable. However, because a large percentage of our payments are electronic, setting up an automatic, expenditure tracking system is the most efficient way to go about it.

To create an automatic expenditure tracking method, use the one-card method by placing all your daily purchases on a singular debit or credit card, which allows you to have an automatic method of tracking how you are using your money.

If you go the traditional route of using cash, maintain a system that allows you to know how much you are earning and spending on a daily basis. This will help you take immediate control of your financial life and future. The essence of tracking your spending is so that you can have a firm and clear idea of the current state of your present financial life.

Step 2

Now that you have a very clear idea of your monthly income and expenditures, the next step is to concentrate on a few key areas. Fixed monthly expenses are your most important expenses. These include expenses such as mortgage payments, car/consumer loan payments, rent, home (e.g. utilities), car insurance, minimum credit payments etc.

To get out of debt, you need to make saving and debt repayment a fixed monthly expense, i.e. you need to dedicate a specific sum of your income to repaying debt, and saving, first by creating an emergency fund, and then by saving to invest towards your financial goals.

How much you choose to dedicate to savings and debt repayment will largely depend on your current income to expenditure ratio and your financial goals. The more money you can dedicate to this bucket (savings and debt repayment), the easier it will be to get out of debt and onwards to financial freedom. For instance, if you can dedicate $1000 to savings and debt repayment—50% saving, 50% debt repayment—each month, you can manage to pay off $30,000 in debt every 5 years.

Step 3

You now have very clear idea of how much money you are earning (after tax), and how much of it you use every month and in which manner. You have also decided how much of your money you will dedicate to repaying debt each month.

Now that you have this data, the next step is to determine whether you need to make some changes and sacrifices. If your monthly expenditure exceeds your monthly income after taxes, you need to consider making some cutbacks and sacrifices in the bigger, key areas of your life.

For example, if you are living from paycheck to paycheck and rent eats up a significant portion of your fixed income expenses, you may consider moving to a cheaper place or area.

To dedicate more to debt repayment, find areas in your life where you can make sacrifices depending on your current financial state and goals. For instance, if things are very tight, you can save more by packing home-cooked lunches and saving that $10. That $300 per month can go a long way towards helping you repay debt faster.

Unnecessary expenditures are great areas to implement cost-saving measures. For instance, if too much of your money is going towards entertainment, limiting how much you spend in this area of your life and then directing the balance to debt repayment and savings can enable you to achieve much more.

When cutting out unnecessary expenditures, you will need to be aggressive. As you look at your list of expenditures, question how much you dedicate to each bucket of your life—50% to needs, 30% to wants, and 20% on savings and debt repayment is the recommended percentage ratio—and what you can do to cut costs so that you can have more money to dedicate to debt repayment and savings.

On the matter of how to prioritize your expenses so that you can find more areas to cut out unnecessary expenditures and thus have more to dedicate towards savings and paying off debt, the most important thing you need to keep in mind is that expenses fall into two categories: needs and wants. Make sure your needs and wants are well below your earning potential, which is how you ensure you are living within your means and are thus in complete control of your financial life and future.

You should now have a budget and identified the amount of money you can reasonably dedicate to repaying your debt. Given the intended aim of this guide is to help you repair your credit, the next thing you need to do is know your credit score. The next chapter talks about that.

Chapter 3:

Improve Your Credit Score

You have prioritized your expenses, reduced your unnecessary expenditures, and where you found it necessary, you have made sacrifices meant to better your financial wellbeing. You are in a good frame of mind because you have created an effective budget that allows you to allocate your income to important areas of your life depending on your financial goals, and to track spending from one month to the next.

By dedicating a specific amount or percentage of your income to debt repayment and savings/investment, you have also made great strides and can comfortably move into the next step.

Your credit score and how it is calculated

Before you start paying off your debt using the specific amount of money you have chosen to direct to that undertaking each month, you need to know your current credit score and more importantly, the important factors that determine your credit score.

Let's start with the basics:

What is my credit score and how is it determined?

A credit score is different from credit history. Credit history is simply a collection of all your debts or financial transactions within a specified account. Your credit score is a three-digit-number, between 300-850, and assigned to you to indicate your likelihood of repaying debt or rather, fulfilling your financial obligations.

The lower you are on the spectrum, the worse your credit, the riskier you are as a debtor, and the less likely you are to get favorable credit rates. The higher you are on the spectrum, the more attractive you are to lenders, and the likelier you are to get loans at very favorable interest rates.

Your credit score comes from your credit history. Your FICO score, which is the most used credit score, normally depends on factors such as your debt repayment history, the amount of money you owe individual lenders, and the type of credit you have.

Repaying debt consistently helps improve your credit score primarily because as you pay off your debts one after the other, your credit history improves and so does your credit worthiness.

How to know your credit score

There are various ways to get your credit score and it is very important that you do so right now, so that you know where you stand and how much work you have to put in to repair your credit score.

The easiest way to check your credit score is by checking with your bank. Most banks offer free, annual credit score checks. In fact, with some banking institutions, to check your credit score, all you have to do is log into their online portal.

If your banking institution does not offer a free credit score check, you can use various tools to get a free credit score report. According to The Fair and Accurate Credit Transactions Act of 2003, the three main credit bureaus, i.e. TransUnion, Equifax, and Experian, should give you a free credit score report every year.

A collaboration between these three credit bureau entities led to the creation of the website AnnualCreditreport.com. Visit the platform to get your free credit score report.

Knowing your credit score is fundamentally important to your journey towards being debt free. If your score is too low, i.e. a credit score of 580-619, start doing everything in your power to ensure that you are repaying your debt as consistently as you can and paying your debt with every single dollar you can spare. The faster you get out of bad debt, the faster it will be to attain financial freedom and peace of mind. An excellent credit score is a credit score of 700 to 850.

Now that you know your credit score, you can get started on improving it. The first thing you need to know about the process is that it is gradual and prolonged. Repairing your credit score may take years—depending on your level of debt and your history in making payments on that debt. If that is the case, the most important thing to keep in mind is that you should repay your debts one at a time, generally focused on the debt with the highest interest rate, consistently until you have no debt and can save and invest more.

That noted, there are very specific strategies you can use to repair your credit score and improve your financial life. Let us now discuss the most effective of these strategies.

Strategies Guaranteed To Help Improve Your Credit Score

You can improve your credit score by:

1. Setting up automatic payments on all minimum debt payments: If you have any debt that requires you to make a minimum monthly payment, make sure you have these types of payments on an automatic system so that you <u>always repay your bills on time</u>. Remember that a large portion of your credit score shows how reliable a borrower you are; the more consistently and timely you repay your debts, the better your credit score.
2. Monitor your CTR: Your Credit Utilization Ratio (CTR) is the ratio of your current credit balance credit limit relative to your credit limit. The lower your CTR, i.e. the lower your rate of using your available credit limit, the better your credit score. To optimize your CTR, <u>ensure that your debt to credit limit ratio is as low as possible</u> by ensuring you are mindful and careful enough not to maintain high debt balances.
3. Pay off debt: <u>Paying off your debts as consistently as possible</u> is the ultimate way to repair your credit score and rapidly progress towards financial stability and freedom. The more debt you manage to pay off each month, the closer you get to being debt free and attaining financial freedom.

This book advocates being very aggressive towards debt repayment. Immediately after figuring out your credit score and how much of your income you can dedicate to debt repayment, get started on the process immediately and aggressively paying your debts with any extra money you have.

There are, of course, plenty of other strategies that you can use to repair your credit; these deserve to be mentioned—especially the third one—because the tried, tested, and proven-to-work way to get out of debt is by repaying it consistently.

In some cases, perhaps in the case of identity theft or cybercrime, you can also dispute a credit score. For instance, if after asking your bank for your free credit report/score, you notice payments that you did not make, you can call the bank to dispute the score and report.

When disputing a credit report or score, keep in mind that the process is relatively simple as long as you can identify the mistakes, report them to your bank or credit bureau, and then allow time for investigations. If your dispute has merit, it should reflect on your credit report/score.

Now that you have your credit score, and are aware that the best way to better your credit score is by repaying your debt as diligently as you can from one month to the next, let's talk about what you can do to start paying off debt in a structured and effective manner that gives you peace of mind.

Chapter 4:

Repay Debt, Improve Your Credit Score, And Become Financially Free

Again, the more aggressive you are towards paying off debt, the faster you will get out of debt, repair your credit score, save, and invest more so that you can move towards financial independence as rapidly as possible.

This chapter covers various strategies you can use to get out of debt faster. Let's start with the most important bit:

How to Get Out of Debt Faster

To get out of debt faster, all you really need to do is:

1. Ensure that you are paying all your debt minimums. The less debt you accrue, and the less interest you have to pay on your debt, the

easier it shall be to pay off all your debts and become debt free.

2. Above paying the minimums, increase your monthly minimum payments because being comfortable with paying the minimum means getting out of debt will take longer and cost you more. Pay monthly minimums on all your debts except one, which you will pay with every penny you can save. The higher your monthly payment, the faster you will get out of debt, repair your credit score, and become financially stress free.

3. We often buy things on credit because we do not have the funds for it. For instance, if your car breaks down, and you do not have ready funds that you can use to repair the car, you are more likely to use credit to have your car repaired because it is an important tool. To ensure you do not accumulate more debt, work on creating a healthy emergency fund; an emergency fund is a great safety net tool.

In respect to which percentage of your income should go towards debt repayment, the percentage will depend on your aggressiveness towards debt and the factors driving your reason to get out of debt. For instance, if your desire is to get out of debt as fast as possible, you are likely to dedicate more to debt repayment than say, someone who has adopted a casual, leisurely stance towards debt repayment. With that noted, the widely accepted recommendation is that you should direct at least 20% of your after-tax income to debt repayment and savings.

Other effective ways by which to lower your debt include negotiating for lower interest rates, restricting credit card usage, consolidating your debt, trimming your budget, or you can sell things you do not need or use and direct the income influx towards debt repayment. Again, the more you can dedicate to debt repayment without necessarily compromising your wellbeing or quality of life, the faster you will get out of debt.

When talking about debt repayment, I cannot fail to discuss debt prioritization and which debts are ripe for consolidation; let's do that now.

Debt Prioritization and Consolidation

The primary question behind debt prioritization is, "which debt should I pay off first, or, in which order should I repay my debt?"

Above making minimum payments on all debts, the most effective advice is to go with what feels right to you. In general, there are four main ways to determine which debt to prioritize and pay off first.

1. The first method is to pay minimums on all other debts and hit the smallest debt with every nickel, dime, or dollar you can save.
2. The second debt prioritization strategy is that of concentrating on paying off the debt that has the highest interest rate as fast as possible. This prioritization method is especially effective because it keeps the amounts you pay in interest low.
3. The third prioritization strategy is to concentrate on paying off the largest debt and then moving down the line until you are at the smallest debt and well on your way to being financially free.
4. The fourth method is debt consolidation so that you only have to worry about paying off one debt instead of multiple payments to different debts. Now that we are talking about debt consolidation:

What is debt consolidation and which debts are suitable for consolidation? Debt consolidation is exactly what the name suggests: consolidating several loans into one loan, a loan that in most cases has a lower interest rate or flexible repayment terms.

The key thing to keep in mind is that debt consolidation does not directly reduce your debt. What it really does well is consolidate your debt under one umbrella so that at the end of the month, you do not have to make several debt repayments.

That some consolidated debts offer lower interest rates is but a bonus.

Another fundamental thing to keep in mind is that debt consolidation may not be possible depending on your level and state of debt. To see if you qualify for a debt consolidation loan, ask your financial institution about it and be especially mindful of the interest rate because a debt consolidation loan is only effective if the interest paid on the combined credit outstanding is lower than what you would have normally paid had you continued paying off your debt individually.

The most common ways by which to consolidate debt is asking your banking institution if they offer credit transfer facilities, capitalizing on a home equity loan, asking your banking institution if you qualify for a debt consolidation loan, or to consolidate your loan by borrowing debt consolidation money against your life insurance policy.

Irrespective of which of the four, debt repayment methods you employ, you need to ensure that you have in place an effective tracking mechanism that allows you to track how you are progressing towards paying off all your debt and becoming debt free.

To create such as system, the first thing you need to keep in mind is your financial goals and the method you use to track your debt repayment plan. Tracking can take many forms. For instance, to track your debt repayment plan, you can use any capable money tracking software, app, or a custom spreadsheet.

As you track your debt repayment—and budget—also keep in mind your financial goals and your progress towards their achievement. Align your debt repayment plan with your financial goals. For instance, if the idea is to get out of debt as fast as possible so that you can start saving for a house, keep this goal in mind and align your credit repayments to this aim.

On setting financial goals and targets, your budget and living below your means are your most important allies. Keep in mind that the more you save and direct towards debt repayment, the faster you will get out of debt, and start building wealth, which is the next step of your credit overhaul and financial freedom plan.

Chapter 5:

Start Building Wealth

The path to building wealth starts with taking stock of where you are, which includes taking note of your debts and creating an effective debt repayment strategy, something this guide has already shown you how to do.

Now that you are paying off debt one at a time and from it, feeling more in control, do not ease off. As each debt disappears and you feel more financially empowered, start thinking about your financial future, your financial goals, and the wealth you need to create to achieve your desired financial future.

In this chapter, I shall discuss potent wealth creation strategies that will help you become financially stable and stress free. I shall start by discussing how to create an emergency fund:

How to Create an Emergency Fund

First, an emergency fund is a sum of money saved and specifically dedicated to covering unexpected expenses such as home appliances repair, emergency home fixes, a prolonged sickness, or unemployment.

To create an emergency fund, start by deciding how much money you would like to have in your emergency fund account. The generally accepted recommendation is to consider your total monthly expenditures and save at least six months of expenditures; so, if you spend $5,000 per month, your emergency fund should have at least $30,000.

However, and with the above noted, what percentage of your income you dedicate to creating an emergency fund will largely depend on your current financial state. If you are struggling to make ends meet, start by setting aside a smaller emergency fund goal. For instance, aim to have $3,000 in your emergency fund account in 3-6 months.

On the question of where to keep your emergency funds, since accessibility is the most important element to keep in mind, direct your emergency funds into a liquid asset. For instance, you can invest your emergency funds in money market mutual funds/ETFs or in liquid certificate of deposits.

On the matter of the percentages to dedicate to debt repayment, creating an emergency fund and saving, aim to dedicate at least 20% of your take home pay towards this endeavor. How you allocate the percentages further will largely depend on your financial aims. For instance, if repaying debt as fast as possible is important, and 20% of your take home pay is $1000, you can dedicate 50% of this sum ($500) to debt repayment—above all minimum debt repayments—and 25% equally to savings/investing and creating an emergency fund.

While we shall shortly discuss invaluable investment strategies that will help you build wealth, a key thing to keep in mind is that you cannot build wealth if you do not have money to invest: *investing is how you build wealth and become financially free.*

Here is a sampling of the best wealth creation strategies:

1. Do not save for the sake of saving. Save so that you can achieve something. Create clearly defined financial goals that motivate you to work towards their attainment. When your financial vision is clear, you will be much more capable of taking the steps necessary to bring about your desired financial future.
2. The more money you have in savings, the more you can invest. If you are pinching

pennies, and struggling to get out of debt, the fastest and easiest way to start building wealth is to reduce your expenses. By reducing your major expenses, you will have more money left to pay debt, save, and invest. If you are struggling painfully, consider things such as selling your car and using public transit—or using your car and your free time to earn some money through ride sharing services—and moving to cheaper accommodations. Once you make such sacrifices, do not give in to the temptation to direct the freed-up money towards buying more things you do not need. Remember that the more money you save and invest, the faster you will get out of debt and started on the path to financial freedom.

3. Start a side business. If you have a salaried, 9-5 job, consider getting a second job or direct your time, money, and effort towards creating a side business that generates income. Starting a second stream of income is an especially great way to create wealth because if you are budgeting your money and living within your means, you can direct any extra income towards debt payment, saving and investing, which effectively helps you build wealth faster.

4. Save with investing in mind. For instance, say, "I will save $1,000 in the next 3 months

and direct these funds towards buying a low cost index mutual fund or ETF." When you save with investing and wealth creation in mind, it makes saving easier because your resolute aim keeps you motivated. Think of your 1, 3, 5, and 10-year financial goals and then save and invest with these goals in mind. For instance, if your desire is to invest in home ownership in the next 5 years, knowing the cost of your dream home will allow you to know how much you need to earn, save, and invest each month to be able to afford your dream.

5. Above all else, diversification is the most important element to wealth creation. Having multiple streams of income allows you to experience financial peace of mind. Consider investing in various areas of interest or creating multiple businesses. For instance, you can start a blog, become a freelance writer, and start a drop shipping business. In such a case, having several streams of income gives you more financial maneuverability.

Wealth creation or generation, especially from an investment perspective, is a vast topic that we cannot cover fully within the confines of this book. The most important thing to note about using your savings to create wealth is first to save with a goal in mind and then to direct the saved money towards creating extra streams of income or generating compound interest.

Chapter 6:

Align Your Mindset

You have heard it said that wealth is a mindset; it is. If you have a poor mindset, you will never achieve wealth. In fact, a poor money mindset is the cause of debt and money problems because when you have a poor money mindset, your relationship with money will also be poor.

To ensure that you keep consistently paying off your debt, saving, and directing your savings towards worthwhile investments, you need to change your relationship with money, which means you need to adopt a new money mindset.

In this chapter, we shall discuss the various things you need to internalize and make habitual so that you can create a positive money mindset that allows you to remain committed to long-term debt repayment and maintenance, diligent saving, and informed investing.

How to Have a Wealth and Healthy Debt Mindset

To create healthy relations with wealth and debt:

Decide the kind of financial life you want

Create a list of all the things you would have if your financial life were perfect. Think of all the things you want and write them down on paper with exact or rough estimates of how much each item will cost. This does two things; the first is that it allows you to strike off your list of things you think you need but that after careful consideration, realize you do not need. The second thing is that it allows you to save and invest with specific goals in mind. It allows you to save and invest towards attaining important financial priorities, which helps you remain motivated towards the debt repayment and wealth creation endeavor.

Delay financial gratification

Credit card debt is often a result of unplanned or impulse purchases. Instead of buying—on credit at that—something shortly after experiencing the urge to do so, delay the purchase for a few days and if after 5-10 days, you still need the item, consider budgeting for it in your monthly budget. The ability to delay immediate gratification for longer-term gains is the most important money management strategy.

Think of it in the following terms. When you delay immediate financial gratification, for example, forgo buying $10 worth of coffee and instead of directing that $300 per month to debt repayment, saving, or investing, you are essentially choosing to "experience pain" now so that you do not have to experience the pain in the future.

The anticipation that builds as you forgo little financial pleasures for bigger exhalation when you pursue and achieve your major financial goals will keep you on track and help you create a healthy relationship with debt and money.

Align your emotions and financial goals

This goes back to what has been the call behind this book: to save towards attaining specific goals. Since the general idea is to dedicate at least 20% of your take home pay to debt repayment, saving, and investing, how much you save and dedicate to debt repayment will largely depend on your emotional goals.

If you feel more motivated to work towards debt elimination before you go all out on saving for larger financial goals such as a home purchase, dedicate a significant portion of the aforementioned percentage to debt repayment so that you can get out of debt faster.

To create a healthy relationship with money and wealth, you need to keep in mind that the emotions you attach to money determine your relationship with it. If you have positive emotions towards money, your financial goals, and debt, you are more likely to have a thriving financial life.

Do not undervalue a budget

In combat, the person, team, or country that wins the war or battle is the one that has the best intelligence, strategy/plan, weapons, and whose soldiers are most determined.

In getting out of and managing debt, saving, investing, and creating wealth, your budget will play a critical role, which is why you should create and realign it as often as possible depending on your primary financial goals.

Most people often develop a negative attitude towards money management and wealth creation because in essence, financial management is about adhering to a budget. Most people often fail to realize that a budget is in its very nature fluid and therefore open to changes as often as necessary. If maintaining a monthly budget is a big hassle, maintain a weekly or even daily budget. That way, you will have a clear idea of your financial standing, and out of this clear idea, you will be able to take action depending on your current financial state and aims.

Budgeting—and consistently balancing and realigning your budget—gives you control over your money, and when you feel more in control of finances, your financial stress decreases as your wellbeing improves.

Conclusion

As this guide has shown you, getting out of debt and overhauling your credit score is not as difficult as most people make it out to be. In fact, there are only several steps to it:

1. Take stock of your debt by listing all your debts on paper in whichever order—low balance or high interest rate.
2. Evaluate your monthly income and expenditures and from this, create a budget that allows you to know how much money you direct to each important area of your life.
3. To get out of debt faster and start creating wealth immediately, dedicate a specific percentage of your monthly income to the undertaking. As noted, this percentage depends on your present financial state and needs, but you should aim to direct at least 20% of your monthly take-home-pay towards debt repayment, emergencies/ emergency fund, and saving/investing. Play around with your percentages until you find what works for

you. The important thing is to commit to paying all you debts on time each month.
4. Hit one debt—it can be the smallest balance or debt with the high-interest rate—with every nickel and dime you can spare and continue going down or up your list of debt until you are serving your last debt.
5. Once you create an emergency fund and have enough left over to invest, do not let your money rest in a conventional savings account. Invest your savings/monies in worthwhile ventures such as ETFs, low cost index mutual funds, crowd-sourced real estate, and other investment options that allow you to generate an additional income. By doing this, you will get out of debt faster and create the critical mass you need to attain financial freedom.

Thank you again for buying this book!

I hope this book was able to help you to overhaul your credit.

The next step is to take immediate action in the strategies laid out in this book.

Finally, if you enjoyed this book, would you be kind enough to leave a review for this book on Amazon?

Thank you and good luck!

Bonus: Checklist

Here is a checklist of the various things you need to do to create a budget and improve your credit score:

Budgeting Checklist

1. Track your spending
2. Use the 50/30/20 budgeting percentage rule to allocate your after-tax income. 50% of your after-tax income should go towards fixed expenses, 30% should go towards wants and other expenses, 20% to debt repayment, saving, and investing.
3. If you are living above your means, find new ways to make money or make tough sacrifices such as moving to a cheaper home, selling off your car, etc.
4. Maintain your budget consistently depending on whether you have a daily, weekly, or monthly budget.

Credit score checklist

1. Get your annual, free, credit score report from the three main credit bureaus: Equifax, TransUnion, and Experian.
2. If you notice suspicious transactions on your credit report/score, dispute it by calling your banking institution.
3. If possible, and where doing so means lower interest terms, consider consolidating your loans.
4. To conserve your Credit Utilization Ratio (CTR), maintain a low debt to credit limit ratio or ask your banking institution to increase your credit limit.
5. Start paying off debt as aggressively as you can. The idea here is to do more than pay the minimum on the debt you have chosen to concentrate on whether it is the smallest debt or the debt with the highest interest rate.

www.ingramcontent.com/pod-product-compliance
Lightning Source LLC
Chambersburg PA
CBHW030735180526
45157CB00008BA/3180